Walt Disney
Pinocchio

GRAFTON BOOKS
A Division of the Collins Publishing Group

LONDON GLASGOW
TORONTO SYDNEY AUCKLAND

There was once a wood-carver who lived in a pretty little house in a sleepy old town. The wood-carver made clocks, musical boxes, and all sorts of toys. His little house was full of the most beautiful things you could imagine.

The old wood-carver was called Geppetto. One day he took a very fine piece of wood and made a puppet.

He was a real marionette, with strings and joints. Geppetto made clothes for his puppet, and even gave him a hat. Then he painted his face. As he worked, Geppetto wondered what he might call the puppet. He decided to name him Pinocchio.

'If only my puppet was a real boy,' Geppetto wished as he went to bed. That night a fairy spoke softly to Pinocchio: 'Little puppet made of pine, wake, the gift of life is thine!' As he came to life, a cricket jumped out of his hiding place.

'Why weren't you at school?' she asked. Pinocchio hid his face in shame. 'I.. I..I met someone,' he blurted out.

'Yes..um..two big monsters.. with green eyes!' As he spoke, something strange started happening to Pinocchio's nose.

'And they tied me up in a big sack!' he went on, his nose growing even bigger. 'And then,' he cried, 'they chopped me into firewood!' At once his nose grew like a tree. 'Oh, my nose!' he shouted. 'What's happening?' 'Perhaps you haven't been telling the truth,' said the fairy. 'You see, a lie keeps growing.'

'It grows until it's as plain as the nose on your face.' At this Pinocchio promised never to tell lies again. 'I'll forgive you this once,' the fairy said, and touched his nose with her wand. It went straight back to normal. The cage sprang open, and Pinocchio and Jiminy got out of the wagon as fast as they could.

'Am I a real boy?' asked Pinocchio. 'No,' replied the Blue Fairy. 'To make Geppetto's wish come true, you must prove yourself brave, truthful and unselfish. Then one day you *will* be a real boy. And you, Jiminy Cricket,' she went on, 'must help Pinocchio choose between right and wrong.'

Pinocchio went dancing round the room, and the noise soon woke Geppetto. 'I must be dreaming,' he thought when he saw the puppet.

Geppetto took him in his arms, and Pinocchio told him about the fairy. 'Soon I'm going to be a real boy!' the puppet said.

Grafton Books
A Division of the Collins Publishing Group
8, Grafton Street, London W1X 3LA.

Published by Grafton Books 1986
Copyright © 1986 The Walt Disney Company
Produced by the Justin Knowles Publishing Group
9 Colleton Crescent, Exeter, Devon EX2 4BY
Edited by Neil and Ting Morris
Designed by Sally Boothroyd

British Library Cataloguing in Publication Data

Pinocchio. — (Walt Disney's Family classics; v. 1)
823'. 914 [J]   PZ7

ISBN 0-246-13081-4

Printed and bound in Great Britain by
Purnell Book Production Limited, Member of BPCC Group

After the show they set off in Stromboli's wagon for the next town. 'Bravo, Pinocchio,' he shouted. 'You are sensational!' 'You mean I'm good?' the puppet asked. 'Good?' said Stromboli. 'Soon your name will be on everyone's tongue!'

Stromboli smiled, 'We will tour the world!' he said. 'Paris, London, Monte Carlo. You will make lots of money...for me. And this will be your home, where I can find you always!'

And with that Stromboli threw Pinocchio into a cage and locked him up. 'No! Let me out!' cried the puppet, but it was no use.

All this time Geppetto had been looking for Pinocchio. He couldn't rest, and searched day and night for his puppet son.

Jiminy was at the puppet show,
and now he came to help his friend.
'I'll soon have you out,' he said,
but the lock wouldn't budge. Just
then the Blue Fairy appeared.

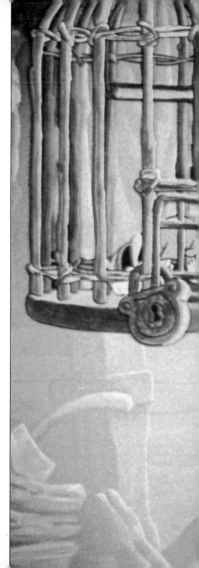

On his way home
Pinocchio bumped
into the fox again.
'After what you've
been through, you
need a holiday!' said
the fox. 'Here, take
my ticket to Pleasure
Island. The coach
leaves at midnight!'

The fox led Pinocchio to the coach, and it set off full of other boys. 'M'name's Lampwick,' said the boy sitting next to him.

'Pleasure Island's a great place,' said Lampwick. 'No school, no cops, you can tear the joint apart, and nobody says a word!'

'Let's go into the rough house and pick a fight!' cried Lampwick. 'Why?' asked Pinocchio. 'Aw, just for the fun of it!' came the reply. Meanwhile Jiminy, who had sneaked a ride to Pleasure Island, saw the coachman with his donkeys. 'You boys have had your fun,' he snarled. 'Now you must pay for it!' 'So that's it,' thought Jiminy. 'I must warn Pinocchio!'

'Where do you think all the kids have gone?'
Pinocchio asked Lampwick. 'Aw, they're round
here somewhere. Who cares, we're having a
good time, ain't we?' 'Sure!' said Pinocchio.

'So this is where I find you,' cried Jiminy.
'Smoking and playing pool!' Lampwick just
laughed. 'Laugh, go on, make a jackass of
yourself,' said Jiminy.

'To hear that beetle talk, you'd think something was going to happen to us,' laughed Lampwick. But as he spoke, he grew donkey's ears. 'Does he think I look like a jackass or something?' he asked.

'You sure do!' cried Pinocchio. At that Lampwick laughed again, but the laugh turned into a loud hee-haw! 'Did that come out of me?' he asked. 'Help! Hee-haw! Hey, beetle! Hee-haw! Hee-haw!' It was too late. Lampwick was a donkey.

Pinocchio was changing too. 'Come on, quick,
let's get home to Geppetto before you get any
worse,' Jiminy shouted. And so off they ran, as
fast as they could.

Back at Geppetto's
house a dove dropped
a message. 'It's about
your father,' said
Jiminy. 'It says he
went looking for you
and was swallowed by
a whale named Monstro.
But he's still alive,
inside the whale!'

'Hey, where are you going?'
shouted Jiminy. 'To find my father!'
Pinocchio shouted back and was
gone. He ran all the way to the
sea, stood at the top of a cliff,
tied his donkey's tail round a
heavy rock, walked to the edge,
and jumped. The rock took him
right to the bottom. 'Can you
tell me where to find Monstro
the whale?' he asked politely,
but the fish looked scared and
darted off.

Pinocchio wondered if Jiminy had followed him, but he didn't have long to think. Suddenly there was a gigantic rush of water, and the fish swam off as fast as they could. But Monstro was faster, and Pinocchio could feel the huge open jaws behind him.

He was sucked backwards and whizzed past the sharp teeth. Inside the whale it was like a vast dark cave. Pinocchio grabbed the tail of the nearest fish, and hung on. Then, to his amazement, he saw the fish hooked by a fisherman's line.

It was Geppetto!
'My boy!' he yelled,
throwing his arms
around him.
'I came to save you,'
Pinocchio said, and
even the wood-carver's
cat was pleased.

'I've got an idea,'
said Pinocchio.
'Let's light a fire
and make Monstro
sneeze. Then we'll
get on your raft
and he'll sneeze us
out into the sea!'

They set fire to all the wood they could find, and it was not long before they felt a rumbling from the whale. They waited on the raft, then suddenly...whoosh!

Monstro started sneezing and off they went, through the dark cave, past the sharp teeth, and out into the sea. They paddled as fast as they could.

Monstro was furious as he charged after them. A great wave washed them from the raft. Geppetto begged Pinocchio to save himself. 'Swim for shore, son', he said weakly. But Pinocchio grabbed his father and pulled him along. Again Monstro charged, and a huge wave threw them ashore. Geppetto was safe, but Pinocchio lay there as if dead.

Geppetto carried Pinocchio home. Then
he knelt down beside his bed and cried.
'My boy,' he wept, 'my brave little boy!'
But as Pinocchio lay asleep, the fairy's
voice could be heard far away. 'Prove
yourself brave, truthful and unselfish,
and one day you *will* be a real boy.'

'Awake, Pinocchio, awake!' said the voice. A twinkling light surrounded Pinocchio, and slowly he opened his eyes, sat up and looked around. Then he looked at himself. 'Father,' he said, 'I'm alive!'

'And I'm...I'm real!' he said, 'I'm a real boy!' It was too good to be true, but it *was* true. 'A real boy!' Geppetto shouted, hugging him and dancing round the room. 'Then my wish has come true!' Jiminy Cricket watched from his old hiding place as father and son danced. 'When you wish upon a star,' he said quietly to himself, 'your dreams come true.'

Pinocchio was curious about everything around him. He specially liked the flickering candle. 'Oh, pretty!' he said, picking up the flame. Geppetto ran across the room. 'You've certainly got a lot to learn,' he cried, and ducked Pinocchio's burning finger in the fish bowl. 'First thing in the morning, off you go to school!'

Next morning on his
way to school, Pinocchio
met two strangers.
'I'm going to school!'
he said proudly.
'School, ah yes,'
said the fox. 'Then
you don't know the
easy way to success!'

Pinocchio shook his head. 'I'm speaking, my boy, of the theatre,' said the fox, eating Pinocchio's apple. 'Why, you're a born actor.'

'Follow me,' he went on, 'to the Great Stromboli Marionette Show!' And before he knew it, Pinocchio was on his way.

Stromboli was very pleased with the new arrival, and soon made him the star of the show. 'Introducing,' he shouted to the audience, 'the only marionette who can sing and dance without the aid of strings!'

Pinocchio sang, and Pinocchio danced. He was still a bit shy with the girl marionettes, but he danced with them and did his best not to make a fool of himself. The audience laughed and clapped and shouted for more.